Enjoy your
Adventure by

Making it so . . . . .

Robert Jan Boonstoven

*"Only through life,
by making it so,
can you ever be."*

Aristotle

MAKING IT SO

by Robert Van Laarhoven

V COMMUNIQUE BOOKS

Copyright © 1998 by Robert Van Laarhoven

Library of Congress Cataloging-in-Publications Data
Robert Van Laarhoven, date.
p. cm.

Making It So, by Robert Van Laarhoven

ISBN 0-9661255-0-9

Printed in the U.S.A

Illustrations and editing by Dana Danielson
Book Cover Design by Yvette Edwards

🙠 *Appreciations* 🙢

My life has been filled with so many interesting and fascinating characters who have brought love and understanding — others who have tested my temperament. They have played many roles in my movie. Each has done so with such intensity and commitment that, upon reflection, I would have dearly missed them if they hadn't done their part. In my youth I misperceived their valuable lessons. Presently, I understand more and appreciate the characters that appear in my movie. To thank all of them at this time would not be appropriate and very time consuming in paper and ink. I do at this time want to thank those individuals who have sat closest to me in the theater and who have shared the majority of my movie so far.

I would like to thank Mary Wolf (Dobeck) for her consistency and marvelous story telling. She reminds me of Meryl Streep in the movie "Out of Africa" where Robert Redford's character would routinely leave on his adventures and return to Meryl's sanctuary to hear her read a heart warming story. I would like to thank Jay Donlin, who over the years has been a gentleman and an inspiration. He was one of the first "Making It So" comrades who, without much hesitation, grasped and incorporated the theory.

I would like to thank my family — from my parents to my eight siblings. One can only imagine what kind of dynamics and humor is possible from being raised in such a large family. I would like to thank Richard Papenfuss, Ph.D., and Phil Wilson, Ph.D., who were very inspiring and kind to me while I tested my wings. Their thoughtfulness and confidence propelled me when I felt stagnate. I would like to thank Jim Elliot whose cool and collected demeanor made my youth enjoyable. I would like to thank the "Dobeck Clan". Their keen sense of humor and spiritual guidance kept me on the path when I was wandering. Roger Knauf, Mark Sproul, Scott Habeck, John Mielke, and Bob Wetstone for your consistent warped sense of humor — I thank you.

I want to thank Robin Johnson for her "deep level of goodness."
Thank you.

Table of Contents

As You Raise The Consciousness Of Individuals Through Numerous Modalities . . .

Inversely Proportional Exits: Poverty, Illness, And Negative Thought Patterns, That Hinder Mankind.

— R. Van Laarhoven

Introduction . . .
MAKING IT SO!

Making It So can seem like it's a balmy 72 degrees in the head all the time.

I have observed through my lifetime many individuals who have suppressed their feelings, desperately attempting to hide their fears. These individuals are not enjoying the process of life. Some of these individuals have hidden behind prescribed medications, alcohol, tobacco, and other drugs, only to cover the hurt and distrust as a painter would in attempt to cover rust on metal. It may have a pretty finish but eventually it will erode and the rust will reappear. They superficially attempt to heal the hurt through numerous modalities that only treat the effect, but do not discover the cause of their pain.

Several contemporary solutions (psychotherapy, 12 step programs, Betty Ford Clinics, etc.) have made many advances, but still have not assisted at a deep level in resolving the core issue. Their advances have assisted individuals to become aware that they can be in charge of their emotions and perceptions. They stop blaming others and realize they are responsible for their actions. This awareness has inspired many individuals to acquire the knowledge that they have the freedom to choose to think and react differently.

Once a person realizes he/she has a choice, it empowers them to believe that they can manipulate their world. They'll set goals and acquire objects in a proud response that they are in control of their world. This will only perpetuate their cycle of desperation; futilely trying to control their world without feeling a sense of true happiness. They will again seek additional help in an effort to feel better about themselves and whatever they are venturing to accomplish in their life.

Many psychologists will agree that the number one reason people come to see them is that their patient feels a lack of control over their world, or they feel "out of control."

Through experiences, wisdom from maturity or a revelation, many individuals come to realize that what they were really seeking all along was to just feel good about themselves while these uncontrollable situations were occurring in their lives. They want to know that everything is going to be **OK**. Or, have the ability to keep their sanity when Mother Nature enforces its power, when their financial world crumbles, when a loved one is ill or has died, or when they feel betrayed by someone they trusted. Others will explain the extraordinary events that occur in their life (sudden death of someone, miraculous life-saving event, lottery winnings, etc.) as a miracle or a divine intervention. They will turn to God to explain the unexplainable. If those individuals would observe over a lifetime the subtle nuances that occur each moment of each day, they might recognize that each action and event is a well-plotted, planned course — as though you were fulfilling a destiny.

An acquaintance once told me a profound statement; "Everyone is seeking three things: one, to be loved; two, to have the ability to love someone or something; and three, to be respected for doing both." I wish I could remember his name and give him credit. It is a powerful and wonderful thought. This book is my attempt to assist others in their discovery to love themselves or love whatever, hopefully to be loved in return, and be respected for possessing both! Recognizing the fact that each individual is fulfilling a destiny that affects millions of people by their participation will be their greatest love. Restoring your health, mentally and physically, will be a by-product.

Different titles were suggested for this book. The title, "Making It So" was chosen for several reasons. One was William Shakespeare's quote, "There is nothing either good or bad except that thinking makes it so." Another was from the Star Trek/Next Generation series. In the series, the Captain of the spaceship Enterprise, in an attempt to resolve a situation, would inform his staff of what steps were needed to be taken. He would then turn to his colleague with precise information and astute confidence and say, "Make It So, Number One." The person who received and trusted the instructions would then move with such grace and fearlessness that no one could impede their progress.

I offer this book with information that you have probably already heard. I am asking you to make it your reality. For students, teachers, writers, speakers, business men or women and/or other professional people, this could be the newest tool to make your life easier, more enjoyable, and lead you to a sensation of "enthusiastic contentment."

Imagine that everything you think, do, and say is in perfect order. Because of your participation, your thoughts and actions will create a rippling effect that will affect millions of people positively.

If you knew this to be true, wouldn't you walk with your head held high, with confidence and fortitude, knowing how important you are?

> "Man is a god clothed in rags. He is a master of the universe going about begging a crust of bread. He is a king prostrated before his own servants, a prisoner walled in by his own ignorance. He could be free! He has walked out of his self-constructed prison, for none holds him but himself."
>
> — *Paul Twitchell*

FULFILL YOUR DESTINY!

*This book will assist
in your evolution from
your thoughts,
to trusting your feelings,
to being your authentic self.*

career, loved ones, money, past thoughts or belief systems. Our world is in a constant state of flux or change. Even you are constantly evolving and changing. Your body is being replaced every 6 months at a cellular level. Your thoughts a decade ago have changed significantly in comparison to today!

When I watch the water in a stream, it tends to flow ever so gently. Sometimes it serpents from one side of the bank to the other, as though it were in a dance with the dirt, rocks and terrain of its environment. As I have observed people who enjoy dancing, it tends to lift or change their spirit. I have never witnessed a person who has danced to be depressed. By moving through our life gently, as though in a dance with our emotions, events, and thoughts, we will eventually perfect it as two beautiful dancers move across an elegant dance floor.

And how do we go gently down the stream? The third part of the song: "merrily, merrily, merrily, merrily," would mean we do it joyously, happily, and with such enthusiasm that we become merry.

The final part of the song: "life is but a dream," is so important that it affects our every thought. Without finding comfort in this phrase, we will eventually find life a burden, chaotic, a struggle to compete, defending and judging our environment. We will be lending ourselves to a feeling of isolation. There are a number of belief systems we can "buy into" (rationalize) in our world. This perhaps is just another one to add to the list, though this one brings me great harmony, understanding, fluidity, and a sense of oneness with the world.

You may have heard someone who is really enjoying the process of their life say, " . . . I couldn't of dreamed it was possible!" It is as though they were living a fairy tale. Then there are others who state that they previously dreamt about the events that are presently occurring in their life when they were a child. Believing and then becoming consciously aware of how your dream/destiny is being fulfilled will bring you unexplainable joy. Once I discovered this was possible, it started to change my thoughts, it changed my perceptions, and then it changed my actions. Was the world changing, or was my perception of the world changing?

This information has been around for millenniums. I was just beginning to understand by opening my mind to what already existed. I started to discover that life was cyclical. We are born into this world as infants, needing to be nurtured and looked after by a nurse, physician, mid-wife, etc. If we then live to a ripe, full age, eventually at the end we are again nurtured and looked after by similar individuals

(nurses, physicians, etc.).   What we do in the interim, upon reflection, will seem like a dream. I was very fortunate to work in an environment that educated me at a young age to benefit from the knowledge of my elders. I worked several years in a cardiac rehabilitation program. These survivors of cardio-impairments would share and bestow their wisdom upon me. Some would mention that if they could do it all over again, they would enjoy their youthful days more–slow down and smell the roses. They would enjoy their relationships more. Try a different career. Spend more time with their children. Nurture the significant individuals in their life. Definitely stop chasing Mr. Green Backs. But the most consistent variable, the most important common denominator, was their wish to have simply "enjoyed life more."

Enjoy your life!

Number one, Make It So!

God Is Playing To An Audience That Won't Laugh

A physicist once described to me that we are unaware of the amount of different radio waves constantly bombarding our bodies. There are short and long band, low and high frequency radio waves. With the recent addition of mobile telephones, you can only imagine how much more our bodies are being impeded. The physicist went on to say that if we were a powerful enough radio receiver we would be able to pick up any amount of information we want to by dialing the tuner into that particular frequency. To me, the most fascinating point was the fact that we had the potential to pick up *anything* with a powerful enough receiver!

The present technology of computers and the Internet can be utilized in a similar manner. Once connected to the Web, the Internet allows you to receive any information you choose. Name a topic, person or thing and the Internet will provide you information on that subject. Our minds also work in a similar pattern. Whatever we choose to focus our attention on, we will receive that information. Let's say you want more information on becoming a physician, there are a plethora of schools and institutions that will provide you with the knowledge to become a physician one day. If we want to become a politician, scientist, beautician, actor, mechanic, entrepreneur, inventor, etc., all we have to do is tune our receiver in by asking someone who is knowledgeable in that profession, simply dialing the telephone and asking for directions, going to the library, connecting ourselves to the Internet, etc.

If we can concur on the previous paragraph, then we know that we are responsible for the information we choose to listen to and read about. If you want to hear about how the world is being destroyed, there are numerous books, articles, and individuals that will support you in your quest for that information. If we want to read about heroic individuals, constructive communities, wonderful philanthropists and thoughtful, inspiring authors, there are also numerous books, articles, and individuals that will support your quest.

Do you remember ever dreaming about what you read or watched just before falling asleep? A scary movie somehow worked its way into your dream. The same can occur when you read a book or watch a soothing, delightful movie. What we consume in our intellectual diet we eventually perceive as our reality. In my previous book, "A Guide to 'Auspiciousness' ", I discuss the ability to alter ones' present thought patterns (radio waves) and observe ones' life in an auspicious, fortunate manner. It is quite remarkable when a person changes a singular thought or belief, how the perception of their external world changes.

A great author, Francis Marie Arouet (Voltaire), said, "God is playing to an audience that won't laugh." As I mature in life, I recognize how important this quote is to my well being. There are so many ways to view the world we live in. Each person is defending why they choose their actions. They have rationalized in their minds lists of reasons why they should be angry, disheartened or apathetic with their world. They may even have a support group that acknowledges their reasons to sustain that belief.

The great playwright, William Shakespeare once wrote, "There is nothing either good or bad except that thinking makes it so." This is a very powerful and intimidating sentence if ones' view of the world is black and white. When a person graduates to an understanding that "thinking makes it so," he/she grasps the nuances of each situation that life brings as an opportunity to judge it either as good/bad or perhaps, by maintaining ones' objectivity, it just **IS**. Do you recall what you did 10 years ago today? That day was probably as important as today in your mind and, most likely, you do not remember it. We have an opportunity to perceive, or observe whatever we choose in our lives. What radio frequency are you choosing to tune into?

In the movie "Parenthood", the father (played by Steve Martin) is distraught by all the distractions and tribulations he and his family are going through. The grandmother consoles him with a remarkable anecdote. She refers to people viewing life as either a rollercoaster or a merry-go-round. Neither is bad or good, it just depends on which ride you enjoy.

Enjoy your life!

Number One, Make It So!

TUNING YOUR RECEIVER

For simplistic reasons and maintaining a continuity with the previous chapter, I am going to describe your mind and body as an electronic metaphor, a "radio receiver". The receiver is an excellent metaphor for several reasons. A radio receiver receives signals via radio frequency waves. These signals are then interpreted by transmitters. Depending on what frequency wave the receiver is tuned into will determine what information you will hear. Our bodies break food down into chemicals. Some of these chemicals react with receptacles (neuro-transmitters) in the brain and then these transmitters can be utilized to interpret data by the brain. How efficient and powerful the receiver is will depend on the quality of the components in the receiver and the clarity of the signal. Likewise, the efficiency and power of our mind will depend on how healthy our diet/body is and how focused and clear our thoughts are!

If you are eating a healthy diet and exercising, you are off to a great start. You are building a quality receiver that can absorb numerous types of signals. On the other hand, if you have a poor diet, you are nonfit, and use alcohol, tobacco, or drugs, you are diminishing the quality of the receiver. To assist your understanding on how to make your body even more efficient, an excellent book to read is Covert Bailey's "Fit or Fat."

The ability to focus our minds and be aware of our thoughts can be challenging, unless we are practicing mind control methods; meditation, tai chi', etc. One is not always aware of the amount of information constantly going on in the mind. If we could write down each thought, each moment of each day, we would be extremely amazed at the amount of energy consumed on what might be called "wasted thoughts". An excellent scholar, Deepak Chopra, discusses this phenomenon in his book, "Quantum Healing". He describes that between each thought there is a space. Depending on how many thoughts you have in a certain time period will limit the amount of space between those thoughts. Dr. Chopra describes this space between thoughts as "silence". Only when there is silence can we hear what the Universe/God is clearly saying. Albert Einstein has been quoted for many things, but one of my favorites is, "I want to know God's thoughts ... the rest are details."

Becoming aware of our thoughts can be an intimidating experience. Once cognoscente of the chatter, we recognize that the noise is usually fear based or ego driven and that taking steps to clarify our mind can seem threatening. The ego of the mind does not want to give up control! It rather enjoys the dictatorship it possesses. But by realizing how limited and fragile the ego is, in comparison to realizing God's thoughts, would be like a raindrop, where pure joy is entering the river.

Fine-tuning our receiver is an art in itself. Balancing your diet, exercise, what you read and observe, how we interpret the information in our life, who we spend our time with, and taking time out to be silent and hear what the Universe/God has to say, can seem overwhelming. When it seems like that to me, I merely recognize that simple tune; " Row, Row, Row your boat, gently down the stream, merrily, merrily, merrily, merrily, life is but a dream." Then I remember that I just have to *enjoy* the process while I balance my life.

Enjoy your life!

Number One, Make It So!

WHAT KIND OF MOVIE HAVE YOU WRITTEN?

There are numerous theories, doctrines and religious beliefs to describe why humans exist. A very interesting and educated man described one theory to me which made me feel ever so delightful, yet fascinated. It tied numerous theories of the ages together: questions of why we exist, where are we going, why déjà vus occur, does reincarnation really exist, is there a heaven and hell, is there a supreme being, what is my purpose or destiny? There are so many questions that it could make ones' head spin. Of all the rationalizations that humans have imagined to answer these questions, the theory that this individual described to me makes the most sense: "Life is just a movie that we have come to participate in." William Shakespeare even stated, "All the world's a stage and all the men and women merely players. They have their exits and their entrances and one man in his time, plays many parts."

Physicists are starting to agree that we could be living on a continuum, a hologram that could exist for eons. The theory that we live on a continuum would mean that we hypothetically exist in the year 15 BC and the year

3003 AD at the same time. This would substantiate the theory of reincarnations and déjà vus, why we dream about foreign lands, characters, dying, being born again, traveling through space, etc. It may be difficult to comprehend due to the fact that we limit our minds to three dimensional thought, and believe we only exist on this planet, earth. If some of you feel this could be getting a little bizarre, hang on, as if you are reading about an interesting movie.

We can address these questions and answer them from a scientific perspective, or we can address them from an artistic view. By indulging myself in the theory that life is just a movie and I have come to participate in it, I needed to address a few questions. Is there a supreme being, a God, if you will? This scholar who described the theory said, "the God could be a singular entity or a collective consciousness." He went on to say that "this God has great love and understanding, of which we are always a part, and grants us anything we could imagine. We are only asked to return that love, as children return to their parents for comfort and joy. There is no demand to return the love, but an awakening by choice to return the love to be a part of God again."

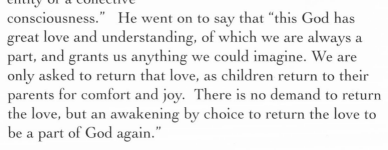

The theory included that our imagination and creativity allow us to create whatever we choose. We have an option to travel to this planet and live by its simple rules. The theory goes on to say that we pay an admission and then participate/observe the movie pre-written for us. God and you chose to write a fascinating story that would encompass all the attributes and sensations of the human experience. Remember, this was done out of free will. You can leave any time you choose, or you can enjoy what was written for you to experience. It is as though you paid your admission to the theater and you are watching a movie on the screen that you selected. You have the option to leave the theater at any time. For me, I already paid my admission, bought the popcorn and beverage, found an excellent seat and have come with several friends to enjoy the movie together. At times I wonder where the movie is going, why these characters are in this particular scene, and then, through patience, it all makes sense for the story line to continue.

When I relate this theory to my life and reflect on how I have written my life up to this point, I become very intrigued. I've been an exciting and interesting writer so far, and can only imagine what I have written for my future. We sometimes have doubts as to where we are going and what is going to occur. Psychics are here to assist us. If you have ever been to one, they simply tell you that eventually everything is going to work out for the best. What else could there be! You have been a fascinating writer and things are always working out for your best interest. Otherwise you probably would not have written it! Enjoy your life!

Number One, Make It So!

WHAT KIND OF WRITING STYLES HAVE YOUR FELLOW COMPANIONS WRITTEN?

O nce you understand and appreciate your writing style, you realize through maturity the kind of writer you enjoy to read and observe. You discover through numerous modalities what kind of music, poetry, authors, playwrights, producers, speakers, preachers, painters, sculptors, sports figures, co-workers, etc., you find to your liking. You discover individuals or groups that think like you, as though you resonate with the person or the object of your focus. You find great comfort when you find a person who shares your beliefs and interests. These individuals or groups have a similar writing style and have come to enjoy the movie with you.

You have chosen the characters in your movie, and in turn, they have chosen you for their movie. Some of these characters we may call parents, siblings, friends, co-workers, business partners, spouses, rivals, and even enemies. They add to the zest of your story line. Without them, the story is not worthy of your participation. We spend so much energy trying to change the persons in our life, we forget that if they did change, it would change the entertainment of our remarkable story. Rod Serling wrote an interesting series of screen plays for television. They were called "The Twilight Zone." One of episodes he had written, portrayed during the late 1950's or early 1960's, was of an accountant at work observing the female staff enjoying themselves, laughing and giggling, by the water fountain. He was very distraught over their lack of productivity in the office. Grumbling under his breath, he returned to his apartment later that day and wondered what the world would be like if everyone was as productive and frugal as he. A knock at the door would answer his question. A package had arrived that contained a book that would grant him his wish to change anything he so desired. He made his wish and the following day everyone on the transit train, and office, was him in appearance and attitude. His world became a very productive and orderly world. The accountant was very pleased and praised how efficient the world had become. No one was laughing or disturbing him at his work. As the day progressed, he found himself quite isolated. Everyone was so productive they had no time for an ordinary conversation. The work environment became unbearable and at the end of the day he raced home to read the book again so he could reverse his wish and return things to the way they were. The following day everything had returned back to normal except for one thing. The friendliest person at the water fountain was the accountant!

The transition from appreciating your writing style to observing and appreciating others is an act of great love and understanding. It is as though you have become a third party in a two way conversation; observing, objectively, how you are interacting and how the other person is responding. You begin to appreciate your needs and the needs of the one with whom you are interacting with. Once you acquire this ability and start to practice it often, you will feel and empathize how extraordinary and creative other writers are in this world. You will discover that if you were in their shoes and living their life, you would most likely make the same decisions. Maybe having judged them prematurely, you now have found a kinder and more consoling thought for their well being. You grow more with wisdom and remember that their well being is a reflection of you. You begin to recognize and validate the famous adage, "what you see in others you possess as well."

The more you read, travel, and observe with over 5 billion other authors, by rowing your boat each day, your life becomes an exceptional journey of entertainment. Fulfilling our story, by actively participating and expressing ourselves with confidence, we recognize the vital role we play for our movie and others. This confidence can offer a sense of bliss. Imagine that everything you do and say is beautiful and worthy. Rebezar Tarz, a great Tibetan monk, wrote: "True happiness is a sensation of momentary balance. When man remembers who, and what, he really is, he does no wrong and injures no one. Even his worst mistake turns out to help others, and they become a profitable lesson to all." Enjoy your life!

Number One, Make It So!

FOLLOWING SIMPLE GUIDELINES ON THIS PLANET

This planet we live on has some very simple rules and guidelines in order to enjoy our pre-written movie. We understand that gravity plays an important part in solidifying our bodies. It is the glue that keeps our particles of matter together and grounded to the surface of the earth. As things are in a constant state of flux, your body/mind and the planet are constantly changing. This flux is consistently changing through polarity (the movement of an attracting positive charge repelled by a negative charge). The sun, through a massive turbulence of energy, repels its energy to earth, while the composite of earth is drawn toward the sun. This assists in the rotating speed of our planet and the distance maintained from the sun. The polarization of the North Pole and South Pole, through the heating and cooling of our planet, assist in weather changes. Our body's voluntary and involuntary muscles contract based upon the movement of positively and negatively charged ions. It may be due to these factors that we as humans have chosen a vocabulary that consistently reflects that polarity. Tall or short, big or small, good or bad, sad or happy, wealthy or poor, etc. It helps us define our world.

Understanding that we are in this constant state of flux, we realize that it is necessary for our survival. If we agree that it is necessary for our survival, then why do we judge our lives or only focus our attention in terms of a negative experience? Living on this planet requires that what goes up must come down. What may be our greatest asset, may become our nemesis. Your enemy could become your ally. What money can do for you, could also destroy you. This idiosyncrasy of polarity, if not understood and respected, can lead to an emotional rollercoaster. If one does not balance his/her diet, work or play, extracurricular activities without rest, and/or sustaining negative thoughts about themselves and their world, one's body will divorce itself and become ill. Dis-ease of the mind will create a dis-ease of the body. A wonderful and wise author, Louise Hay, has written a splendid book "How To Heal Your Body." She describes with simple examples how your thoughts affect your body. Ms. Hay also gives examples of correcting those thoughts and curing the disease by countering ones' negative thoughts with positive affirmations. It is a tremendous collection of simple examples how the polarity, if unbalanced, can challenge your enjoyment of the movie.

Making It So

This polarity includes fear and love. An astute author, who remained anonymous, ascertained that we have only two thoughts; one based out of fear and the other out of love. When I reflected upon my thoughts, and broke them down to their simplistic form, I too recognized that they were either based on fear or love. This author went on to say that neither of these thoughts were good or bad but that love seemed to give us more energy and enthusiasm towards life. It made the journey of life more enjoyable. This person also described how love can accumulate. The image of a glass (human spirit) and water (love thoughts and deeds) were used as a metaphor. Each droplet of water reflected a choice of love, while fear was not the opposite, or took away the droplet, it just represented nothing. It was as though the energy to think in fear was nonproductive. Each time you thought of and/or acted upon a loving thought, it added a droplet to the glass. The goal was to fill the glass to the brim as an investment program. Eventually the investment would return significant benefits/dividends to the investor. Once reaching the brim of the glass, it took only one more loving thought or action to break its seal. When the seal is broken with that crucial droplet, the water begins to overflow, and the abundance of love never again equals the singular droplet of love added to the glass. Once the person is committed to sustaining loving thoughts, the rewards for their efforts/investments is the self-realization of their purpose and destiny on this planet.

Successful movie goers tend to possess an attitude of love and graciousness. They have accepted that they have a choice to perceive events in their world as good or bad. They appreciate the fact that the movie is going to go on with or without their cooperation. Their responsibility is to either gently row with the current or paddle against it. Once they have found the techniques to balance their day to day activities and enjoy the journey, life becomes quite a spectacular event. The movie will be over before you know it.

Enjoy your life!

Number One, Make It So!

INTERACT WITH YOUR SOUL/MIND/BODY AS THOUGH IT WERE A MENU ON A COMPUTER SCREEN

Your character in this movie is very diverse. You require the balance of your nutritional, physical, social, emotional, intellectual, financial, and spiritual needs. How to juggle and balance each of these needs can seem overwhelming. Indulging too much into either of these categories will neglect the others and create an imbalance.

Each category can be viewed as a menu from the software on a computer screen. The mouse/modem allows us to select that program or category. For hypothetical reasons, let's say we selected from the menu the category of "intellectual needs." This program is intriguing and stimulating. We can become captivated by this program for a great deal of time. We may even become over stimulated by the program to a point where the program locks up and we are unable to exit from this category. This intellectual selection has psychologically disrupted the balance we previously desired. What seemed to be a fun and useful tool is now working against us. We may need to see an expert in finding our way out of the program. A psychologist, an expert in the field of balancing intellectual needs, will assist in our return to the main menu. The same becomes true of the other programs. Over indulging in food, physical activities, social endeavors, and spiritual quests can create a narrow and limited movie screen. The movie is still going on but our view has been impaired and less enjoyable.

We are always given warning signals by the computer that indicate to us: "are you sure you want to do this?" "the battery is running low," "there is an error in this program," etc. There are signals given to us each moment of our day that assist us in the progression of our movie. We sometimes become so consumed by the events or situations that we override the warning signals. We continue to stay in that selected program past the recommended "pleasant" timeframe. There will be acute warnings in your health, physical pain in your body, disruptions in your relationships, and/or emotional anxieties. If you continue to override these warnings, over time they will become chronic. Again, there is nothing wrong with these program selections and overindulging in each category. Remembering that even our worst mistake is a benefit for all. It just depends on how you wrote your story and if you are enjoying the process. I am writing this only to assist you in becoming cognoscente of our world. I enjoy movies about healthful, energetic, imaginative characters who have overcome their limitations on this planet and who have found levity in their everyday lives. Others may and have preferred a variety of scenarios that do not include these adjectives in their movie. I do appreciate their diversity and this book may not offer much to them.

Checking in periodically to find a balance between these categories helps me recognize humility when I find myself taking one of them too seriously. Lovingly expressing and admitting when I have overindulged in a certain category is quite uplifting. It seems to make friends out of strangers. The musician Jim Morrison wrote "people are strange when you are a stranger." Expressing yourself honestly and sincerely is the greatest form of love. By holding in our thoughts, we suppress our gift of fulfilling the movie for ourselves and our companions. Children express the truth when they are young and some are taught to suppress their real feelings. How confusing to such a young soul! Truth and honesty will lead to clarity, and clarity will always lead to happiness. I love the quote from Spencer Tracy: "Remember your lines in life and don't bump into the furniture." Have you found your modem? Have fun selecting all the great programs that are available.

Enjoy your life!

Number One, Make It So!

ONCE YOU DISCOVER YOU CAN HAVE WHATEVER YOU WANT, WHAT'S NEXT, ANOTHER GOAL?

An inspiring author and speaker, Anthony Robbins, educates individuals and groups on how to obtain whatever you want. He describes the power hidden in each person that enables them to focus their energy to obtain whatever they desire. He has inspired numerous people to powerful heights. I have noticed though, that it becomes a perpetual goal-seeking mission. The goal each time becomes a little more difficult to obtain and perceived to be worthy of your efforts. If you have not gone through his seminars or listened to his tapes, at least talk to someone who has completed the course.

If you have completed his course or similar courses, you will find yourself inspired and focused on what you think you desire. It lends itself to a competitive ritual with yourself and colleagues. It has you focusing on your future and not the moment. An issue in goal-setting that I'm aware of is, "what if you do not obtain that goal?" How does it make you feel? Are you rowing your boat gently? Perpetual goal seeking can be exhausting. You obtain a goal, then how long do you enjoy it? The next goal you set is a little more difficult and again perceived worthy of your efforts. The cycle continues, perpetually chasing goals.

An interesting book, written by Trina Paulas, "Hope For The Flowers," is an enchanting story about the pursuit of a goal. It is about two caterpillars who fall in love. One of the caterpillars was intrigued by a mass of other caterpillars climbing a pillar (i.e., "the corporate ladder") that reached high into the sky and above the clouds. Curiosity got the best of the caterpillar and it went in pursuit of climbing the "pseudo-pillar". The goal was to see what was beyond the cloud. On its journey, the caterpillar met other enthusiastic crawlers struggling to climb over each other to reach the top. The caterpillar asked his colleagues, "what is at the top?" No one knew, but they all agreed that it must be something spectacular 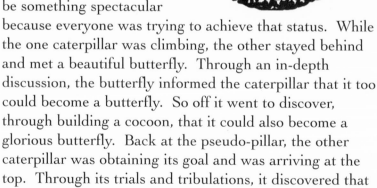 because everyone was trying to achieve that status. While the one caterpillar was climbing, the other stayed behind and met a beautiful butterfly. Through an in-depth discussion, the butterfly informed the caterpillar that it too could become a butterfly. So off it went to discover, through building a cocoon, that it could also become a glorious butterfly. Back at the pseudo-pillar, the other caterpillar was obtaining its goal and was arriving at the top. Through its trials and tribulations, it discovered that there really was nothing there at the pinnacle. It was very disappointed and started to warn others. The colleagues at the top tried to stop it from warning other caterpillars. They did not want other caterpillars to know how foolish their efforts had been. The caterpillar in the cocoon eventually became a glorious butterfly and set off to find the one it loved. Upon finding its companion, sad and perplexed, alone at the top, described this wondrous ability to become a butterfly. The caterpillar fulfilled its destiny and joined its loved one by becoming a glorious butterfly.

The use of a caterpillar as a metaphor in this story wonderfully explains how parallel our lives can be to the destiny of a caterpillar. The caterpillar rows its boat by actively eating leaves day after day. Once they have built their cocoon, it is time to reflect inward, a time of silence. Through time and patience the caterpillar is transformed into a beautiful butterfly. You must know someone who, over time, has been patient and understanding, and the more you get to know them, the more beautiful they become. In the story I also enjoyed how the one caterpillar, who became a butterfly first, patiently waited for its loved one. It allowed the loved one to follow its goal, yet had the wisdom and perseverance to know that eventually it would fulfill its destiny one day.

Goal-setting is another menu choice. If the goal controls you, an imbalance will occur with the other needs of your life. Acknowledging that you are going to fulfill your destiny with or without your cooperation, goal setting can be looked upon as wasted energy. How many people have you met or heard about that, in their pursuit of one goal or several goals, ended up nowhere near where they thought they would be in their life? When that person recognizes this phenomenon, we label it as a serendipitous event. How fortunate and creative a writer we were and didn't even know it at the time.

Enjoy your life!

Number One, Make It So!

THE DANGLING CARROT THEORY!

Why is it when we are pursuing a certain object, person, or thing/goal, it hangs in front of us like a dangling carrot? We'll try anything to obtain this carrot, yet the moment we truly do not want the carrot anymore and go on to pursue another object, person or thing/goal, we find that an abundance of that sought-after carrot is available for us.

When I attended college and studied for an exam, or during an exam, or tried to answer a difficult problem on a homework assignment, my mind would sometimes freeze up, and I would become frustrated. The more I tried, the more my mind would freeze up and the more I became frustrated. When I would relax though, and enjoyed doing something else and later returned to the frustrating situation, the answer soon appeared. The more often I practiced this, the more proficient I became. I would notice that by being patient and enjoying the process, answers would appear auspiciously. The way I was looking/perceiving the issue prior to my frustration, became crystal clear when I would relax, enjoy, and look at it from a different perspective.

I started applying this technique to my everyday life.
During work and play, I would actively pursue something
and when it appeared to be a struggle or my attempts
were being blocked by some unknown reason, I would let
it go and try to do something completely different. I
would then return, look at it from a different perspective
and evaluate it to see if it was worth my efforts to continue
in the pursuit. The more often I did this, the easier and
more proficient I became. Through my research of
pursuing, letting go, and then returning to the pursuit, I
found many of my pursuits not worthy of my time or
effort. There were many times during my period of
"letting go", I would find something more beautiful and
more enjoyable appearing right in front of me, as though it
were a serendipitous event. As I continued testing this
theory, I gained more confidence and trusted to tune my
receiver into the idea of "letting go." I read numerous
books on this subject and talked to others who have also
understood and applied this concept. I started to see a
parallel between "letting go" and becoming cognoscente of
what I truly desired.

During that point of
"letting go," my mind
would slow down as
though I were
consciously meditating.
I started to become
aware of each thought.

I too noticed this space between thoughts as Dr. Deepak Chopra described in his writings. While I was practicing these moment to moment attempts of "letting go" and becoming aware of each thought, information about many subjects and explanations of lifes' questions became clear to me. As though my knowledge of subjects and theories were being accelerated at an increasing rate. I later grew to understand that this space and silence between my thoughts allowed me to focus even more of my energy on the next thought or object. It was as though my mind, before "letting go," was a sprinkler head, spraying water and thoughts across a wide area and by "letting go" and listening, I was able to focus and bring clarity to my life, similar to projecting water from a powerful garden hose.

I enjoyed "letting go" and observing all the options that were available to me in this world. I realized that by disciplining my mind, being cognoscente of each thought and desire, and then focusing on my next thought, I could obtain anything. But what did I truly desire? Each desire had its pros and cons. Each desire/goal took time and effort. By letting go, was I becoming apathetic? Then it occurred to me, I still needed to row my boat. I still needed to be active and participate in the process of enjoying my movie and my fellow companions' movies.

The sport of golf became an excellent metaphor for me. To strike the ball proficiently in this game becomes an art form. When you begin the sport, the distance the ball travels is not always related to the speed at which the club is swung. Many golfers understand this theory. When gripping the golf club, it has to be held as though you were holding a dove. Too gentle, and the dove will fly away. Too strong, and you can injure the dove. Swinging the club should be a fluid movement. This is why they emphasize the words, "stroking the ball." Row your boat with long, fluid strokes. The game is an enigma, it is futile to believe you can perfect this game or perfect ones' life (the only reason we laugh in life is because of imperfections and we all love to laugh). The golfers who enjoy the game the most, I found, were the ones who: understood themselves and their game, utilized course management, understood that where the ball landed was an interesting and challenging position to the cup, and they did not take the game personally. They also understood that there are 18 different holes to play and if they happened to make an errant stroke, it was just another opportunity or challenge to recover and take their next best shot at the game. They seem to remember that even their worst shot was a benefit for all. Foremost though, they merrily enjoyed playing the game with their fellow golfers.

Enjoy your life!

Number One, Make It So!

What Is There Between Each Thought? Are You Listening?

Gurus among the ages have talked about disciplining our minds through numerous modalities. They were attempting to slow our minds down and develop a sense of tranquillity. Recently, the author Dr. Deepak Chopra did an excellent task in explaining the time and space between each thought. He describes this space as "silence" and has stated, "Where there is silence, God is present." In my prior writings, I also wrote about this space between each thought and for me, it was the time to recognize and appreciate the writing style I had written and what my fellow companions had written for our movies with God.

Whatever reason satisfies your interests, being aware of your thoughts and then listening to the space between those thoughts, will be one of the most loving and adventurous events in your life.

Each individual will describe his/her experience of slowing the mind down and becoming more aware of themselves (mind, body, and soul) in relation to their outside environment, in as many different ways as their own special personality. This is why there is no singular divine method of reaching nirvana. There are scientific rationalizations, religious organizations and other spiritual belief systems attempting to recruit others to believe that their personal/groups' quest is the correct one. From, Buddhism to Judo-Christianity, they strongly believe theirs is the way to enlightenment or heaven. They have set rules and laws that control their followers. Depending on how strong of an influence you had as a child, you either enjoyed the belief system of your parent(s) or guardian, or it propelled you in another direction. If you enjoy being controlled and being made to feel guilty, there are plenty of belief systems that will engage your mind to follow them. There are books and theories dated to ensure that their belief system has been around the longest, so it would appear that theirs stood the test of time. Sheer quantities of members would pronounce theirs is the best to follow. One thing is for certain, there are an abundance of belief systems and more developing each day. Check in with your belief system, are you clinging too tightly to a branch or to the shore of the stream?

Are you really listening? What belief system are you buying into? Does it control you through fear or does it give you comfort and love? Does it claim that it is the only and true way? Does it condemn others who do not believe in its beliefs? Does it embrace or push away your fellow brothers and/or sisters? Does

it bring you joy or guilt? If Allah, Jesus-Christ, Buddha, or? is supposed to be a loving God, wouldn't it love everyone it created, no matter what they did? It would be like a parent who loved their child. They may not always like what their child does, but
their love for the child never changes.

> TIME SEALS WITHIN ITSELF,
> TO SAVE WHAT'S RIGHTLY YOURS,
> AND GIVES TO YOU WHEN TIME IS DUE
> THE KEY TO OPEN THE DOOR.
>
> WHICH LEADS TO LOVE
> AND LIGHT
> AND SOUND
> AND PLACES WHERE NO LONGER TIME
> IS FOUND.
> — *Anonymous*

To lengthen the time of listening during the space between each thought will take great discipline. I was fortunate to read a book called "A Course In Miracles" by the Foundation For Inner Peace. The book went through daily affirmations that trained my mind. For 365 days it reconstructed my thought patterns.   Its conclusion was not a means to an end, but a means to begin. It allowed me the freedom to discover my relationship with the universe. I'm discovering it's a fantastic voyage!

Enjoy your life!

Number One, Make It So!

EVERY THOUGHT IS BASED ON LOVE OR FEAR. WHICH ONE ARE YOU PERCEIVING?

In recent times, I have noticed a tremendous amount of energy spent on the subject of FEAR. Stickers on automobiles stating NO FEAR. Books and seminars teaching others on how to let go of fear. Fear itself has engulfed many peoples lives. Marianne Williamson wrote a book called "Returning To Love" and in one of her excerpts from her audiotapes she states, "you mean the devil is in  my head, that is the last place I want it." Ms. Williamson was using humor to help indicate that the devil and other fearful thoughts only exist in our mind.

Fear is only a perception, it exists or does not exist. It depends on the energy we are willing to give it. The twelve step program is a good example. In its attempt to release fear in people's lives, most noticeably alcoholics, it has now trapped these loving minds into believing that for the rest of their lives they will be in the twelfth step. It has become their focal point. Do they have control over the alcohol or is the alcohol still controlling them? They may forever be trapped until they realize that they need to embrace the alcohol. Once recognizing that the alcohol is their friend and it has brought them many gifts (process of learning about themselves, meeting new acquaintances, etc.) they will be free of its control. That act will free their mind to enjoying something else. When there is freedom, rather than being forced to abstain from an object, the mind/body will eventually progress towards a more balanced and healthy alternative.

This can be applied to anything in your life. Find the joy in whatever you are seeking and you will be amazed how easily it appears.

There are teachers who will help you visualize what you are seeking. The most important step in the process of visualization is to already see yourself possessing whatever you are seeking. Truly believing it is possible and seeing yourself having this possession, you will be amazed how it can be manifested into your life. The question remains, did you create this or did you just become aware of your true destiny? You can go through the rigorous methods of desiring, seeking and obtaining until you recognize that these objects will never satisfy your thirst. What will satisfy your thirst will be what you were seeking all along. Self-approval and self-love!

A great author and genuine kind human being, Gerald G. Jampolsky, author of "Love Is Letting Go Of Fear", quoted from the "Course of Miracles", "Forgiveness is the key to happiness". Learning to forgive yourself for your misperceptions and embracing what you thought was unforgivable, will allow you to have a joyous and wonderful life. This is your inherent destiny. What appears to be your nemesis will someday become your ally or asset.

Knowing that I have a tendency to misperceive allows me to have the compassion to forgive myself and, in turn, I understand that others also have this tendency to misperceive and it makes it easy for me to have compassion for them. When I am cognoscente and proceed with love, the person or situation opens up as though it were petals opening from a flower and I am able to share in their beauty. If I had the ability to travel in their shoes, and live through their situations in life, I may perceive it the same way. It reinforces the familiar adage, "people are only strange when I am a stranger." Shirley MacLaine added, "The more I traveled the more I realized that fear makes strangers of people who should be friends."

Love is too wondrous of a word to try to define it. It is too difficult to explain or attempt to give examples. But make no mistake:

> LOVE AND A COUGH
> CANNOT BE CONCEALED
> EVEN A SMALL COUGH
> EVEN A SMALL LOVE
> —*Anne Sexton*

You will always be able to recognize–LOVE. As Mother Theresa stated: "We do not do great things, only small things with great love".

REMEMBER, YOU ARE A SPIRITUAL ENTITY THAT IS HAVING A HUMAN EXPERIENCE!

Dr. David Hawkins has developed a chart that measures ones' consciousness. He has divided this chart into five categories and each category is then divided into levels of perceptions and energy fields. Each energy field is associated with ones' consciousness. Dr. Hawkins developed the energy fields based upon Jesus' shroud on one end of the spectrum and death/suicide on the other. A test of Jesus' shroud was the highest energy force known to scientists at this time. The scale was then adjusted incrementally downward, testing other great scholars, artists, laymen, etc., energy fields and ending at the point where death and suicide gave no energy or it elicited a negative energy. To discover in more detail how he devised this chart or collected the data, one would have to talk to Dr. David Hawkins himself. Through my readings, observations, and scientific research, I find his final conclusions quite interesting and remarkably accurate.

Dr. Hawkins divides human consciousness into categories based upon how they perceive: EMOTIONS, INTELLECTUAL PROCESSES, ACTIONS, VIEW

OF THE WORLD, AND HOW THEY VIEW GOD.
Each emotion is cross-referenced to: how they thought,
how they acted upon those thoughts in everyday
situations, how they viewed the world, and then how they
did or did not view God in their lives. There are nineteen
cross-references and each is given a measurement of the
energy fields each one possesses. An example of a low
energy field would be perceiving to act guilty. The
emotional perception would be to feel *self hatred*, your
intellectual process would be to perceive *destruction*, the
action you took was *guilt*, the *view of the world* would be *sin
and suffering* and you would *view God*
as *a destroyer or hell and fire
forever*. On the other half of
this spectrum, a higher
form of energy would be
perceiving to act
lovingly. The *emotional*
perception would be
feeling *unconditional
understanding, forgiving and
the desire to honor all life*. The
intellectual process would be a
perception of a *revelation*, the *action*
would be to *love* and the *view of the world* would be
perceived *as endlessly supportive and happy*. You would then
perceive to *view God* as an *unconditional and loving God*. The
energy field, based upon Christ/Buddha/Avatar (Dr.
Hawkins utilized these names instead of Jesus' shroud)
being the highest form, was worth 1000 points. The
energy field of "guilt" would be worth 30 points, and the

"love" energy field would be worth 500 points. It is as though, when we dial our receiver into certain perceptions or emotions, it linearly affects other variables in our life that we are not cognoscente of at the time.

Once reading Dr. Hawkins' materials, we can evaluate how we acted upon a situation and cross-referenced it to how we may have perceived the other categories. An interesting phenomenon occurred for me while I was evaluating these categories. I felt more energetic when I started to perceive the world differently. I noticed when I changed my perception, my emotions changed, and my actions towards others changed. It was quite fun. I hope you find it as enjoyable.

I had several friends and colleagues read the theories and concepts I had written up to this point of the book. I asked them what they thought and felt about my writings and to respond candidly. Each person enjoyed it and encouraged me to pursue publishing and promoting it. Each person might have added a comment or two to expand on a theory they found enjoyable. The comments would pertain to what was occurring in their life and generally were inconsistent to a comment from another person, except for one comment. They were concerned with the opportunity to have a choice in life. Did they have the freedom to select or choose what they were going to do or think?

This is actually why I wrote this book. I want people to observe, tune-in, acknowledge the fact if they really have a choice, or are we fulfilling a pre-determined destiny? Are we choosing our thoughts or are we awakening to thoughts given to us from a higher source? I'll give you simple examples. As a child you acquire the knowledge to put letters together to form a word. The words are put together to form a phrase and phrases are put together to form a sentence. These sentences form a paragraph, paragraphs form a page and pages form a chapter and eventually chapters form a story or novel. Does a child create the letters to form words to build a story or did the child become aware of what already existed. You may have walked past several pieces of art and never noticed them. Then one day you became aware of that artwork. You learn to appreciate the beauty of the art. It was already there until you became cognoscente of its existence. I know these are simple analogies but they reinforce the theory that there are no original thoughts. We still quote and embellish what scholars wrote eons ago. "Originality is undetected plagiarism," was quoted by William Inge years ago!

We attempt to manipulate our world and claim that what we invented are new ideas. We find out later that someone had already thought it was possible but were unable to manifest it at that time.

By evolving and trusting your feelings and discovering your authentic self (expression of love)–we realize simply that there are only two choices. To either experience love or fear. The more complex our world appears the more we value the simple things. Enjoyment comes from the pure recognition that everything is either an expression of or a request for love. When one simplifies and evolves, one acquires the knowledge of the fascinating phenomenon: "Is the world changing or is my perception of the world changing?" or as another famous adage says, "Am I singing because I'm happy or am I happy because I'm singing"?

I have learned to appreciate the great individuals who preceded me. I also recognize that I can only appreciate or see in others what I possess. This is why I find another of Voltaire's statement so valuable: "Appreciation is a wonderful thing, it makes what is excellent in others belong to us as well." As I awaken, by opening my mind or tuning in my receiver, in an attempt to understand our universe, I realize how limited my thoughts are–and I become more gracious and humble to the wonderment of our universe! I have evolved to recognize that if I see the world of separation (fear), it will lead me to isolation and illnesses, but if I see the world of oneness (love), I experience improvements in my health, relationships, business and more joy in my life.

If we believe we are spiritual entities and acknowledge that we are on this planet for a very short time, why not enjoy the human experience? The experiences of feeling emotions, how imaginative our minds work, respecting how polarity affects the rhythms of our life and how our earth's force field limits our movement and confines certain elements for our enjoyment. If the theory that our life has been predetermined, why not row your boat gently and enjoy the ride.

Enjoy your life!

Number One, Make It So!

Many people are waiting to be loved – first!
Then they will love.

Why wait – will you love first?

The rewards that come from loving first
are immeasurable.
Those who love first are Making It So!

Your Quest is to Know

If you are in doubt,

simply just ask

the truth will soon appear.

AUTHOR'S NOTE

I hope you have enjoyed this book. If you understand and are applying the theories, you must be having a wonderful time. I am excited to meet you and share in your movie. There will be many others who share in our belief and are as excited to meet you as I am. You may meet some of these extraordinary individuals wearing an insignia along your path. Please take the time to talk to these individuals and share openly and honestly what is occurring in your life. What you have to say and are presently doing will be invaluable at that moment, or it will benefit each of you in the near future. It will be as though you have found an old friend in the movie theater and are sharing an excellent movie experience.

Please write down your thoughts–keep a journal–express your true feelings. Over time, observe how your life has certain patterns/cycles/rhythms to it. Writing these thoughts down will crystallize the movie events and plot the direction of your destiny.

If you would like the "Making It So" insignia and other apparel, please send your request and RSAE to:

V COMMUNIQUE
PO Box 51731
Durham, NC 27717

OR VISIT MY WEBSITE: www.makingitso.com

These are exciting times. The wisdom and appreciation you have gained to understand and live this theory is very remarkable. Make no mistake, you have accomplished great deeds and this is the time to enjoy.

Your alchemy — your highest good, is to enjoy your life without regrets.

May your movie include good health, wealth and love and the time to enjoy them all.

— Robert Van Laarhoven

Room Full of Mirrors

I use to live in a
Room full of mirrors…
All I could see was me
But then love, came on so strong,
That it broke the mirror prison,
She set my poor heart free.

Broken glass use to be all in my head
Jangling, screaming, cutting in my brain
Broken glass was all in my head…
It use to fall out my dreams and cut me
In my bed but love and hope came and saved me
From the dead.

I said how can I ever repay you
She said just remember it's love that will never die
And remember my friend and lover…that sooner you discover,
The sooner our heart's will come alive
And then she kissed and wiped the tears from my eyes.

Song/poem by the guitar legend, Jimmy Hendrix